T0040701

TODAY'S U.S. AIR FORCE

by MICHAEL BURGAN

Consultant:
Raymond L. Puffer, PhD
Historian, Retired
Edwards Air Force Base History Office

COMPASS POINT BOOKS
a capstone imprint

Compass Point Books are published by Capstone,
1710 Roe Crest Drive, North Mankato, Minnesota 56003
www.capstonepub.com

Editorial Credits
Editor: Brenda Haugen
Designer: Alison Thiele
Production Specialist: Eric Manske
Library Consultant: Kathleen Baxter

Photo Credits
DoD photo by Myles Cullen, 16; NASA, 41, NASA/Robert Markowitz, 43; U.S. Air Force painting,
31, U.S. Air Force photo, 7, 33, 39, 40, 42 (bottom), Airman 1st Class Benjamin Wiseman, 27,
Bennett Rock, 21, Capt Tana Stevenson, cover (top), Dennis Rogers, 22, J. Rachel Spencer, 15, Jamie
Pitcher, 20, Master Sgt. Russell E. Cooley IV, 37, Mike Kaplan, 17, Osakabe Yasuo, 6, Senior Airman
Christopher Griffin, 19, Senior Airman Matt Coleman-Foster, 5, Staff Sgt. Christopher Hubenthal,
34, Staff Sgt. Christopher Hummel, 12, Staff Sgt. Joely Santiago, 25, Staff Sgt. Michael B. Keller, 9,
Tech Sgt Michael R. Holzworth, cover (bottom), 1, Tech Sgt. Bennie J. Davis III, 8, Tech Sgt. Jason
W. Edwards, 13; U.S. Navy Photo by PO2 Joan E. Kretschmer, 10; US. Air Force photo by Staff Sgt.
Michael B. Keller, 24, Tech Sgt. Michael R. Holzworth, 28; Wikimedia/U.S. Air Force, 42 (top)

Artistic Effects
Shutterstock: doodle, Ewa Walicka, Kilmukhametov Art, W.J.

Library of Congress Cataloging-in-Publication Data
Burgan, Michael.
  Today's U.S. Air Force/by Michael Burgan; consultant Raymond L. Puffer, PhD.
    p. cm. – (U.S. Armed Forces)
  Audience: Grades 4-6.
  Includes bibliographical references and index.
  ISBN 978-0-7565-4620-5 (library binding)
  ISBN 978-0-7565-4633-5 (paperback)
  ISBN 978-0-7565-4672-4 (ebook PDF)
  1. United States. Air Force—Juvenile literature. I. Puffer, Raymond L. II. Title.
  UG633.B83 2013
  358.400973—dc23   2012023145

Printed in the United States of America in Brainerd, Minnesota.
092012   006938BANGS13

TABLE OF CONTENTS

CHAPTER ONE:
MISSIONS IN AIR AND SPACE

On a dusty Afghan road, a truck bounces along. Men with machine guns ride in the back of the truck. They are insurgents, fighters opposed to the Afghan government and the help it gets from the United States. Miles above the insurgents, a small aircraft tracks every turn the truck takes. The plane is a drone, one of thousands owned by the United States. No pilot sits inside the drone directing its movements. Instead, a camera on board sends images of the truck over thousands of miles, using a satellite even higher in the sky. The images reach a U.S. Air Force pilot at a base in Nevada. Using a computer and joystick, the pilot keeps the drone on course. It's almost as if he's playing a video game—except his work is serious. When the order comes, the pilot presses a button that launches a missile from the drone over Afghanistan. The missile hits its target, destroying the truck.

Just 20 years ago, that Air Force pilot in Nevada may have trained to fly a fighter jet. Or he might have flown a bomber, designed to drop bombs deep into enemy territory. But drones have become the Air Force's weapon of choice as it helps the U.S. battle insurgents and terrorists across the world. The drones can give U.S. ground forces advance warning of enemy movements. They are an "eye in the sky." The drones also fire missiles and drop bombs without risking pilots' lives.

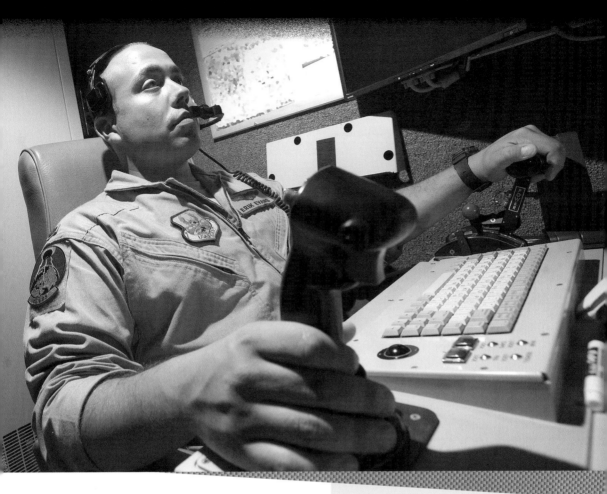

Technology has changed the U.S. Air Force over the years. Pilots once trained on biplanes—slow, wooden aircraft with two wings. By the 1970s pilots flew jets that screamed across the sky at more than 1,500 miles (2,414 kilometers) per hour. Along the way, the Air Force also took control of launching and operating many of the U.S. satellites that orbit above Earth. This branch of the military also operates large rockets that can fly thousands of miles while carrying nuclear warheads—the most powerful weapons in the world. With the increasing importance of computers, the Air Force has ventured into cyberspace. Some Air Force members try to prevent enemies from harming important military computer systems.

A LONG, PROUD HISTORY

In 1907, just four years after the first engine-powered airplane flew with a pilot onboard, the Army created the Air Service to fly the first American military planes. Its first aircraft reached an average speed of about 42 mph (68 kph). The Air Service was renamed the Army Air Corps in 1926, and its pilots set speed records and showed the possibility of refueling planes in flight. In 1941, during World War II, the name changed again, to the Army Air Forces. Its pilots flew fighters and bombers in both Europe and Asia. In 1945 Army Air Force bombers dropped the world's first atomic bombs, simpler versions of today's nuclear weapons. Those missions helped convince Japan to end the war. Two years later the United States Air Force was created as a separate branch of the military. While other branches also fly planes and helicopters, the Air Force has the primary military role in the skies.

The Air Force uses the most advanced technology, but it counts on people to make the technology work. As in the other branches of the U.S. military, the members of the Air Force volunteer for service. They want to serve their country. They believe they can play important roles. As they are told when they enter the Air Force, the volunteers "provide the air and space power necessary to protect America and our way of life."

Along with protecting the United States, the Air Force also keeps the president safe when he flies. It operates Air Force One, the president's plane. And the Air Force does more than fight and defend. In emergencies its members offer assistance to people in need. When earthquakes or other natural disasters strike, the survivors often look up and see U.S. Air Force planes overhead. The planes drop supplies and food. With the power of its aircraft and the knowledge of its crews, the Air Force has many roles to play in a sometimes dangerous world.

Air Force One flying over Mount Rushmore

THE PRESIDENT'S PLANE

Air Force name: VC-25A
Based at: Andrews Air Force Base, Maryland
Range: 7,800 miles (12,553 km)
Speed: 630 mph (1,014 kph)
Number of crew: 26
Special features: Capable of refueling while flying; secure communications systems; medical equipment available for emergencies

CHAPTER TWO:
THE MANY PARTS OF THE AIR FORCE

When most people think of the Air Force, they probably imagine pilots flying planes and helicopters in combat. But in 2012 the USAF had fewer than 4,000 pilots trained to fly combat aircraft, out of an active force of about 333,000 members.

All members of the Air Force, whether men or women, are known as airmen. The title is also used for the 162,000 civilians who work for the Air Force. The Air Force also includes the Air Reserve. Its 71,500 members are not full-time airmen, but they receive military training and fly many of the same aircraft the USAF uses. The Air Reserve also sometimes carries out special missions, such as fighting fires from the sky. And each state and territory has an Air National Guard. The president can order the Guard to work with the Air Force when needed. Since 2001 thousands of members of the Air National Guard have served in either Afghanistan or Iraq.

An airman monitored cameras and radars that tracked boats along the Florida coast.

HURRICANE HUNTERS • • • • • • • • • • • • • • • • • •

One task the Air Reserve handles is weather reconnaissance—observing the movement of storms and collecting information about them. Teams known as Hurricane Hunters carry out the job. The teams are based in Mississippi. They fly along the country's coasts and over oceans, tracking tropical storms before they become hurricanes. The weather reconnaissance teams also collect information about some winter storms. A mission can last up to eight hours. The crew on the plane uses special equipment to measure a storm's strength.

THE ORGANIZATION
OF THE AIR FORCE

A military working dog
helped an airman on
patrol in Baghdad, Iraq.

The Air Force is part of the U.S. government known as the Department of the Air Force, which is part of the Department of Defense. The secretary of the Air Force is a civilian in charge of the department and is named to that job by the president. The department's top military officer is the chief of staff. This general is also one of the Joint Chiefs of Staff, the top military advisers to the president. The Air Force also has a chief master sergeant, who works closely with the secretary and the chief of staff. He or she looks out for the interests of enlisted airmen.

Most of the Department of the Air Force is broken up into large units known as major commands (MAJCOMs). Some commands are organized by regions of the world. One major command, for example, is based in Europe, while the major command associated with the Pacific Ocean is based in Hawaii. A MAJCOM might also be built around the particular role it plays. The Air Mobility Command, based in Illinois, focuses on rapidly sending Air Force equipment and crews anywhere they're needed around the world, along with other jobs. Another major command trains all the new recruits. Separate from the major commands are smaller units that work with all commands or carry out special duties. One of these is the United States Air Force Academy, which trains future officers.

THE THREE TIERS OF ENLISTED AIRMEN

Tier	Ranks
Senior noncommissioned officer (SNCO)	Command chief master sergeant, first sergeant, chief master sergeant, senior master sergeant, master sergeant
Noncommissioned officer (NCO)	Technical sergeant, staff sergeant
Junior enlisted airman	Senior airman, airman first class, airman, airman basic

Each major command is divided into smaller units. One of these is the wing, which usually has from 1,000 to 5,000 members. Within each wing are smaller units called groups and squadrons. The squadron is the most basic unit, with from 50 to 750 members. A squadron's role can range from carrying out combat missions to providing security at a base.

With its size and wide range of missions, the Air Force offers a variety of jobs. Aircraft need mechanics to make sure they are safe to fly. In a combat zone, other airmen have to make sure those aircraft have the proper missiles and other weapons on board and ready to fire. On the ground, airmen have to operate the radar systems that search for enemy planes or weapons. And meteorologists watch for weather conditions that could affect flight missions. Planes, whether carrying people or supplies, have to be loaded properly. Intelligence— the gathering of information—is important

A maintenance crew worked on an F-15 in Guam.

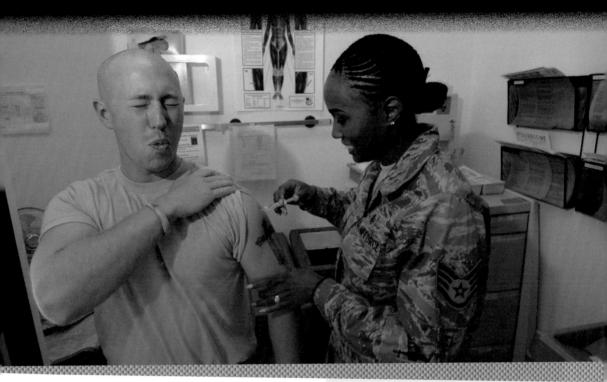

Service members must have current immunizations so they are ready for missions.

for knowing what an enemy might do. Someone has to collect and process this information, then pass it on to officers so they can make the best decisions in the field.

Not everything airmen do is connected to warfare. The Air Force has its own lawyers who work with airmen. These lawyers perform a number of services, including helping airmen who might be accused of breaking USAF rules or U.S. laws. Airmen who have an accident or simply come down with the flu need doctors and nurses to take care of them. The medical staff also makes sure airmen are medically fit for duty. Computers need to be fixed, and ground vehicles need to be in good shape. The Air Force has its own reporters and photographers to help its members know what other airmen are doing. That information keeps the country informed as well. And the USAF even has its own bands, which play rock, jazz, and other forms of music. Almost any job available in civilian life can be found in the Air Force too.

CHAPTER THREE:
JOINING THE AIR FORCE

"We do the impossible every day."

That's the message visitors see when they go to the U.S. Air Force home page on the Web. The Air Force uses the Internet and social media as tools to recruit new airmen. It also has offices around the country where young men and women can learn more about the service. And Air Force recruiters go to a variety of public events to talk about the challenges and benefits of becoming an airman.

A recruit can take one of two paths into the Air Force. One is to enlist. Many recruits join as enlisted airmen right out of high school. The other option is to become an officer. This requires a college degree, but airmen can earn their degrees after enlisting. Both enlisted airmen and officers receive a number of benefits. The Air Force provides training in many technical areas and helps pay for schooling not directly related to Air Force work. In addition, all airmen receive medical care, housing or money to live off base, and food. Family members also receive some or all of these benefits.

Joining the Air Force is not as easy as walking up to a recruiter and asking to be let in. Anyone seeking to join any branch of the military must pass certain tests. One set of aptitude tests measures a possible recruit's math and English language skills. The tests show the Air Force that the recruit has the skills and knowledge to succeed. The results also show what jobs the recruit might be best for.

Along with taking aptitude tests, a recruit talks to a recruiting officer about

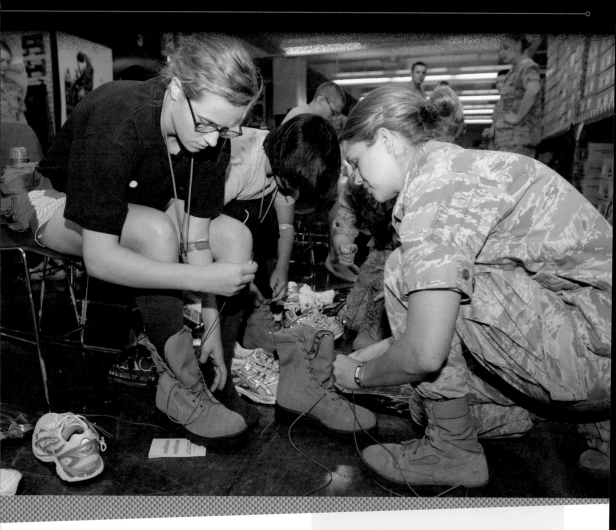

the specific jobs he or she would like to pursue in the Air Force. Then the recruit must pass a physical exam. The Air Force wants to make sure recruits are in good physical health and don't use illegal drugs. The Air Force also has a weight limit, based on a recruit's height. For example, someone who is 5 feet (152.4 centimeters)

tall cannot weigh more than 141 pounds (64 kilograms). At 6 feet (183 cm), the weight limit is 202 pounds (92 kg). Assuming the recruits pass all the tests, they're ready to take the oath and begin basic training.

Cadets marched to lunch at the Air Force Academy in Colorado.

Most people seeking to become Air Force officers can follow one of three paths. A college graduate can apply for Officer Training School (OTS). The school is located at Maxwell Air Force Base, Alabama. As with enlisted airmen, the Air Force has several basic requirements for age and citizenship, and applicants must pass physical exams and aptitude tests.

Another way to become an officer is to join the Air Force Reserve Officer Training Corps (ROTC). This program is offered at colleges and universities across the United States. Potential officers earn degrees while also receiving Air Force training. The Air Force pays for most of the cost, and in return officers promise to serve in the Air Force for at least four years once they finish college. ROTC students, called cadets, must earn good grades to stay in the program.

Finally, high school graduates can earn their college degrees at the United States Air Force Academy in Colorado Springs, Colorado. Cadets, who must be from 17 to 23 years old, apply to enter just as they would any other college. They must be unmarried. If they have children, cadets must legally turn over their care to someone else, often relatives. The four years of schooling are hard, and the Air Force wants cadets to focus only on their training.

Cadets at the Air Force Academy go through basic military training. Then they learn the skills they will need as commissioned officers. All cadets also have a chance to fly some kind of aircraft. After graduation, just over half become pilots or navigators, the airmen who help guide planes in flight. The cadets receive all their schooling for free and collect a salary. In return they agree to serve in the Air Force for at least five years. They enter the service with the rank of second lieutenant. Many stay in the Air Force for 20 or 30 years, earning higher ranks along the way. Many also continue to take classes, adding to their skills as airmen.

A cadet crawled through water on an obstacle course during training.

RANKS OF COMMISSIONED OFFICERS

Title	Insignia
General	Four silver stars
Lieutenant general	Three silver stars
Major general	Two silver stars
Brigadier general	One silver star
Colonel	Silver eagle
Lieutenant colonel	Silver oak leaf
Major	Gold oak leaf
Captain	Two silver bars
First lieutenant	One silver bar
Second lieutenant	One gold bar

CHAPTER FOUR:

LEARNING THE AIR FORCE WAY

Before any airman sees the inside of a combat plane or sits at a radar screen, life in the U.S. Air Force starts with basic training. For enlisted airmen this process is called Basic Military Training. For airmen at the Officer Training School, it's Basic Officer Training. And cadets at the Air Force Academy have their own basic training, while also adjusting to college life at one of the best universities in the country.

The 8½-week Basic Military Training course starts with Week Zero. Incoming airmen receive haircuts, get their uniforms, and begin to learn the basics of drilling—marching in order with other airmen. The goal, as the USAF website says, is to let airmen know "This is not home anymore."

In Week 1 some class work begins. The airmen learn the various ranks and insignias connected with them. Airmen also learn the basics of their first weapon—the M16 rifle. In addition, Air Force life includes keeping clothes and possessions in order at all times. Attention to detail starts with those small things, so airmen will pay the same close attention when carrying out their missions.

During the next six weeks, airmen begin thinking about choosing their career in the USAF. They also learn basic medical care—stopping bleeding or keeping a broken bone steady—and work more with their M16 and other weapons. Preparing for combat is crucial. To the Air Force, its airmen are warriors. They must learn to accept the fact that they might be called on to kill—and could be killed themselves.

Airmen also learn the core values of the Air Force: Integrity First, Service Before Self, Excellence in All We Do. Integrity means doing the right thing in all situations, such as obeying the law and telling the truth. Service Before Self stresses the idea that the airman's needs and wants are not as important as meeting the Air Force's missions and defending the country. And excellence in all actions means airmen do their missions as they've been taught, to make sure no one's life is put at risk for no reason.

Basic trainees stood in formation awaiting orders at the Basic Expeditionary Airman Training course.

Throughout basic training, an airman goes through exercises so his or her body is in the best shape it can be. Airmen also learn about such things as the history of the Air Force, the proper way to act with airmen of higher ranks, and what to do if they are ever in danger in enemy territory. They must be able to survive in the wild and try to evade enemy forces. If captured, airmen should resist giving information to the enemy and look for ways to escape. These steps are known as Survival, Evasion, Resistance, Escape (SERE). Some airmen later receive more intense classes in SERE. When basic training is over, enlisted airmen go to various bases to learn the technical skills they'll need for their chosen Air Force career.

For men and women entering Officer Training School, Air Force life starts a little differently than in basic training. For example, candidates buy some parts of their uniforms and can bring cars to the school, though they have limited use of them at the start of training. But as in basic training, learning to follow orders and respecting higher ranks is important. So is physical training. Within one week of arriving at OTS, candidates must be able to run 1½ miles (2.4 km) and do a certain number of push-ups and sit-ups based on their age, sex, and size. Officers are also

An OTS instructor trained a student on proper saluting.

expected to march and keep their living spaces in order, just as enlisted airmen do.

Basic Officer Training also focuses on the skills officers need to lead others in battle. Officers must work with people from a variety of backgrounds. They must give the airmen they command confidence in their decisions. They must help the airmen under them learn to work together as teams. Many hours of class work help the future officers learn these skills and the ideas needed to conduct warfare.

During the 12-week program, candidates start their day at 5:15 a.m. and are up until about 11 p.m. Exercises test how well they solve problems. After several weeks, they help train new candidates at the school. When the course is over, the students have earned the rank of second lieutenant. They also continue their educations in specific areas, such as flying combat aircraft.

THE AIR FORCE ACADEMY

Cadets at the Air Force Academy go through Basic Cadet Training. On the first day they take an oath, a statement promising to defend the Constitution of the United States. All airmen, including civilians, take a similar oath. Then, for five weeks, the cadets go through physical training and learn about military life, including the need to follow orders and pay attention to detail. Training begins at 4:30 a.m. during "First Beast," the first part of the program. "Second Beast" starts with a 5-mile (8-km) march to a nearby valley. The cadets set up tents, which they live in for almost three weeks. Daily activities in the valley include learning how to use weapons, increasing physical strength, and learning to work as a team. During the five weeks of First and Second Beast, cadets can't see visitors or receive phone calls.

When basic training is done, the cadets start their college careers. But unlike most first-year college students, the cadets must follow many rules. They gain more rights each year at the academy, but they never forget that they are on a path to become officers in the United States Air Force.

Cadets tackled the monkey bars during their basic training.

LEARNING LANGUAGES ● ● ● ● ● ● ● ● ● ● ● ● ● ● ● ● ● ●

Starting with basic training, the Air Force offers airmen the chance to learn many things. In 2006 the USAF opened its Culture and Language Center at Maxwell Air Force Base, Alabama. The center is part of the larger Air University, where enlisted airmen and officers can take a variety of college-level courses and special classes geared toward military issues. The Culture and Language Center gives airmen the skills they need to deal with people from many nations. USAF crews operate in all parts of the world and sometimes work with the military of other countries. The Air Force believes that understanding how people in those countries live makes it easier for airmen to get along with them. Learning the native languages of foreign countries is an important part of that goal.

Perhaps the most visible and respected members of the USAF are the pilots. Pilots and airmen called Combat Systems Officers (CSO) go through special training, if they can meet the requirements. Pilots learn how to fly the most advanced planes in the world. CSOs navigate or operate the electronics and weapons onboard aircraft used to attack enemy targets. A candidate for either position must have a college degree and have earned good grades. He or she must pass a strict vision and health test and meet height requirements—more than 5 feet 4 inches (163 cm) tall but shorter than 6 feet 5 inches (196 cm). Candidates with flying experience have a better chance of entering the program. Students begin their flight training in Colorado and continue to learn for more than a year. After the basic training ends, pilots learn how to fly specific combat aircraft. CSOs go to Pensacola, Florida, to learn specific skills. Some enlisted airmen, such as some engineers and aerial gunners, also receive flight training. But even though flight is a huge part of the Air Force missions, most airmen do their work on the ground.

CHAPTER FIVE:
WEAPONS SYSTEMS

An F-22 Raptor flies toward enemy territory. The fighter carries a cannon and missiles to defend itself against enemy planes. Also on board are bombs and missiles the pilot can launch at enemy targets. To the Air Force, the Raptor is a weapons system—just one of many designed for various missions to defend America.

Here's a look at some of the aircraft, missiles, and space vehicles that make the USAF one of the most powerful military forces in the world.

The F-22 entered the Air Force in 2005. It began replacing older jets, the F-15 and F-16. But all three planes are still flown today. These planes can fight enemy jets or attack targets on the ground. Pilots see information from their planes' computers directly on displays in front of their eyes, so they never have to look down at controls as they fly. Computers help the

F-22 Raptors fly in formation during a training mission.

An F-35 Lightning II joint strike fighter flying over Florida

pilots detect friendly and enemy aircraft and easily fire the weapons onboard.

The F-22, unlike the older jets, has stealth technology. Other stealth planes included the F-117, which was replaced by the Raptor, and the B-2 bomber. In 2011 the Air Force received the first model of a new stealth fighter, the F-35. In the years to come, it is expected to be the main fighter plane for all branches of the U.S. military.

F-35 JOINT STRIKE FIGHTER

Crew: 1
Length: about 51 feet (15.5 meters)
Wingspan: 35 feet (10.7 m)
Height: 15 feet (4.6 m)
Speed: About 1,200 mph (1,931 kph)
Weapons carried: variety of missiles, laser-guided bombs, and mines

TRICKY TECHNOLOGY ·

The United States began working on stealth technology for aircraft during the 1970s. Traditional airplanes have rounded surfaces. The surfaces easily reflect back radar signals, meaning the planes can be detected as they fly. Stealth planes have flat surfaces and many sharp angles. A radar signal hits a stealth plane and bounces off, but not back at the radar system that sent the signal. A stealth plane uses metals that trap the radar signal, rather than sending it back to the detector. Planes can also be detected by the heat their engines create. Stealth technology can include a system to mix engine exhaust with cool air from outside the plane. American stealth planes have given the USAF big advantages over enemy forces. But some military experts warn that new kinds of radar could make it easier for enemies to detect even stealth planes.

Along with fighters and bombers, the Air Force also has what are called attack planes. Their main mission is to fire their weapons at enemy ground forces, to help U.S. soldiers carry out their mission. The two primary attack aircraft are the A-10 Thunderbolt and two versions of the AC-130. The Thunderbolt requires just a pilot, while the AC-130 has a crew of 13. The AC-130 can also carry out reconnaissance and attack any enemies it discovers.

Other important aircraft include the C-5 and C-17 cargo planes, and the KC-135 tanker. Using special equipment, the tanker can refuel other planes while they fly. A variety of planes whose names start with E carry complex electronics into the sky. Their crews can detect enemy targets and help control the movement of U.S. aircraft over battlefields. One of these is the E-3 Sentry, which carries the Airborne Warning and Control System (AWACS). The system can handle communications with ground forces as

Pilots train on A-10C Thunderbolt II aircraft in Georgia.

well as watch over friendly and enemy actions on the ground or at sea. And flying high over enemy land, another plane, the U-2, can take pictures or detect radio signals without being seen. This spy plane has been in use since the 1950s.

Helicopters are also part of the USAF aircraft fleet. The main helicopter is the Pave Hawk, which has a variety of uses. It can be used to search for and rescue downed pilots or help defend ground troops during battle.

The newest type of Air Force weapons system has drawn a lot of attention. The Air Force began flying the Global Hawk drone in 2001, shortly after the September 11 terrorist attacks on the United States. That drone can stay in the air for long periods to provide reconnaissance. At present, though, the military is thinking of getting rid of the Global Hawk, because of its cost. The Reaper and Predator drones also conduct reconnaissance. And both can be equipped with missiles. The Reaper can also carry laser-guided bombs. As the demand for drones has increased, so has the number of pilots. In 2011 the USAF trained more drone pilots than fighter and bomber pilots combined.

From rockets more than 200 feet (61 m) tall to missiles small enough to fit under a plane's wing, the Air Force uses them all. The large rockets can reach speeds of more than 25,000 mph (40,234 kph) and are used to launch satellites into space. The missiles can be used to attack enemy ships, planes, or ground targets.

A special kind of missile is the intercontinental ballistic missile (ICBM). It was first developed in the 1950s to carry nuclear weapons between continents (intercontinental). Today the Air Force controls several hundred Minuteman ICBMs.

PREDATOR DRONE

- First used by the Air Force for reconnaissance in 1995
- First test firing of a missile from the Predator in 2001

Wingspan: 55 feet (16.8 m)

Length: 27 feet (8.2 m)

Height: 7 feet (2 m)

Maximum takeoff weight: 2,250 pounds (1,021 kg)

Speed: Cruise speed around 84 mph (135 kph), up to 135 mph (217 kph)

A Predator drone at Creech Air Force Base in Nevada

They're in cars and even in cell phones. Global positioning systems (GPS) make it possible to find where we're going and always know where we are. At the heart of the systems are satellites circling Earth. The Air Force played a role in developing GPS for military use. It still launches the satellites and helps run the system for both government and civilian users.

Another Air Force satellite system provides long-distance communication for the president and his military advisers during wartime. And the government relies on Air Force satellites to track space launches carried out by foreign countries, in case some might pose a threat to the United States.

At the heart of most modern weapons are complex computers and various sensors. Keeping them safe from viruses or other computer problems is also a key part of the Air Force mission. The Air Force is part of the Department of Defense's Cyber Command, which protects U.S. military computer systems from enemy attack. Efforts in cyberspace also include creating secure computer networks for other countries, such as Afghanistan. The possible dangers of a cyber attack have been known for some time. In 2011 Americans learned that viruses were found on the computers that control many USAF drones. The military did not reveal if the viruses harmed the computers. Detecting and cleaning viruses and other harmful programs will be a major concern in the years to come.

A Defense Support Program satellite detects when missiles are launched.

CHAPTER SIX:
AIR FORCE MISSIONS

The Air Force has changed in many ways in just the last few years, and more changes are coming. In 2012 the U.S. Department of Defense looked ahead to what the military might look like in 2020. Military officials agreed it would be smaller, with less money to spend on new weapons. Yet the Air Force and the other branches would still be able to carry out their missions to defend the country against terrorists and foreign countries seeking to harm the United States.

Within that overall mission, the Air Force has several important tasks. Here's a closer look at some of them.

Along with the U.S. Navy, the Air Force handles the country's nuclear weapons. The entire nuclear force for the country is part of the U.S. Strategic Command. Based at Offutt Air Force Base, Nebraska, the Strategic Command has members from the four major branches of the military, the Air Force, Army, Navy, and Marines. Along with controlling nuclear weapons, Strategic Command deals with issues relating to space, cyberspace, biological weapons, and chemical weapons.

The Air Force has about 450 Minuteman missiles equipped with nuclear warheads at bases in three states. Nuclear bombs and smaller missiles are carried on B-2 bombers and the older, larger B-52 bombers. The Air Force plans to build a new bomber that could also carry nuclear weapons. All the Air Force bombers can also carry non-nuclear weapons.

The launch of a Minuteman missile

Nuclear weapons are considered a deterrent—something that keeps another country from attacking the United States first. An enemy knows that if it used nuclear or other weapons on the United States, it would face a devastating attack from the Air Force's nuclear weapons.

On any battlefield, controlling the skies above is one way to win an easier victory. Air superiority means being able to easily attack the enemy with aircraft, without risking heavy losses. It also means not having to face attacks from enemy planes. The Air Force uses a variety of weapons to achieve air superiority. It also relies on skilled pilots, mechanics, and technical crews—one reason why the Air Force stresses training for its airmen.

Air Force fighter planes are key. They can shoot enemy planes out of the sky or destroy the planes before they can take off. Air Force planes can also attack an enemy's command and control systems, which are needed to get planes airborne and help guide them in flight.

The Air Force counts on the F-22 Raptor and the new F-35 to help give it air superiority. Both planes have more advanced technology than planes produced in other countries. In recent years, however, some Air Force officials have worried that buying fewer of the planes could weaken U.S. control of the skies.

An F-22 Raptor during a training mission over the Nevada Test and Training Range

Air Force drones have given U.S. forces a new way to stay one step ahead of the enemy. The drones can track enemy soldiers or watch over one area for hours at a time. They are a key part of the military's reconnaissance and surveillance tools, which are designed to collect intelligence. With this information, officers can predict what an enemy might do and plan the best way to protect U.S. forces.

The Air Force has an Intelligence, Surveillance, and Reconnaissance (ISR) agency that directs the collecting of intelligence. Within it is the Distributed Common Ground System. At 45 sites connected into a single network, airmen look at the images gathered from drones and larger reconnaissance aircraft.

The Air Force ISR Agency uses satellites and sensors in the ground and underwater to detect if other countries are testing nuclear weapons. Agency airmen also watch over cyberspace to learn if someone is trying to harm U.S. computer systems. The agency also tracks radio communications around the world and tries to break secret codes an enemy might be using to hide its messages.

A SILENT EYE

Flying a Predator drone is challenging. Pilots work with sensor operators, who control a drone's cameras. Other airmen process the information the drone gathers. The drone can capture sharp video images from higher than 10,000 feet (3,048 m)—high enough that the Predator can't be seen or heard on the ground. And sensors on the aircraft can detect heat. Thousands of miles away, the drone's operators can tell if someone has fired a gun because the gun creates heat when it's used. A "hot gun" could mean that an insurgent has just fired at a U.S. soldier. The drone crew can then call for an attack on the insurgent.

SPECIAL OPERATIONS

In every branch of the military, some missions require extra secrecy. They also require specially trained men with the best weapons. The soldiers, sailors, and airmen who carry out these missions are part of the country's Special Operations forces.

The U.S. Air Force Special Operations Command has airmen trained for a variety of missions. They are known as commandos. The most highly trained belong to a unit called the 720th Special Tactics Group. Its members use whatever vehicle or aircraft they need to reach their target—including motorcycles and skis. One job for these airmen is to go into enemy territory to prepare an airfield for U.S. aircraft. The Combat Controllers who carry out this mission have to be prepared to fight if they are detected. Once an airfield is set up, the controllers then guide U.S. planes to the field.

Another Special Operations task is rescuing injured or captured members of the military behind enemy lines. The trained airmen who carry out this dangerous mission are called pararescuemen. Their skills include fighting with a variety of small weapons, parachuting, and treating wounds. They can rescue people from collapsed buildings and find objects underwater. Pararescuemen also rescue civilians in danger because of natural disasters.

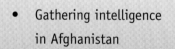

RECENT MISSIONS OF USAF SPECIAL OPERATIONS

- Gathering intelligence in Afghanistan

- Directing aerial attacks on enemy forces in Afghanistan

- Aiding earthquake victims in Japan

Hundreds of satellites circle Earth, and someone has to watch over their movements. The Air Force Satellite Control Network (AFSCN) plays a large part in doing that job. Antennas and tracking stations around the world follow the movement of U.S. and foreign military satellites and weather satellites.

The airmen at the AFSCN do more than track the satellites. They communicate with them and receive

Special ops airmen jumped out of the back of a C-130 Hercules while practicing combat operations in Florida.

information that the satellites send back to Earth. Some of that information includes intelligence used by the military. The center can also track the flight of intercontinental ballistic missiles and rockets used to put some satellites into space.

37

CHAPTER SEVEN:

THEY ARE THE AIR FORCE

You've read about what the Air Force does and the tools it uses. But who are the people who have made the USAF what it is today? Let's take a look at some of the men and women who have played important roles in Air Force history.

Serving in World War I, aviator Billy Mitchell led huge numbers of attack planes against enemy forces. General Mitchell saw how important aircraft would be in future wars, and he conducted a test in 1921 that showed how six large bombs dropped from planes could destroy one of the largest warships afloat. Mitchell also argued for an Air Force separate from the U.S. Army. He didn't live to see that

happen, or to see the heroics of Army Air Force pilots during World War II.

One of the most famous World War II pilots was Richard I. Bong. He flew a P-38 Lightning fighter in Asia and quickly downed five enemy planes in dogfights, earning the title of ace. Bong was known for swooping down close to his target, firing, and then quickly pulling up—key skills in a dogfight. Bong went on to shoot down 35 more Japanese aircraft. His 40 kills are the most ever recorded by a U.S. pilot. He received the Congressional Medal of Honor, the highest award given to members of the military. Back in the United States in 1945, Bong was given

LIFT HERE

a new assignment: to test fly the first jet-powered American aircraft, the P-80 Shooting Star. Bong died during a test flight of the plane.

General Billy Mitchell and his Vought VE-7 Bluebird at an air tournament in 1920

Members of the Army Air Force called the Tuskegee Airmen also played an important role in World War II—and in history. These African-Americans trained for a number of aviation jobs, mainly at Alabama's Tuskegee Institute. The Airmen's fighter pilots had great success protecting U.S. bomber planes over Europe. The Airmen also proved wrong some white Americans who thought that black pilots weren't as good as whites. One Tuskegee Airman who played a part in that was Alva Temple, who flew 120 combat missions. After the war, in the new USAF, Temple and several other black pilots took part in the first "Top Gun" competition. It let pilots of all branches of the military show their flying and shooting skills. The Tuskegee Airmen won the event.

The Tuskegee Airmen in 1943

Astronaut Virgil Grissom prepared to enter the Liberty Bell 7 spacecraft.

When the United States first thought about putting men into space, it turned to the military for astronauts. In 1959 the National Space and Aeronautics Administration (NASA) chose three Air Force test pilots to join the first team of seven astronauts. One of them, Virgil "Gus" Grissom, made the second U.S. space flight. He later died during a test for the Apollo space program, which eventually sent the first human to the moon. Edwin "Buzz" Aldrin, the second person to walk on the moon, was an Air Force fighter pilot before he became an astronaut. A number of Space Shuttle commanders also began their flying careers in the USAF. One of them, Steve Lindsey, announced in 2011 that he would work with a private company trying to put people into space.

After World War II, Air Force pilots often played important roles in testing new, faster planes. The greatest test pilot of all was Captain Chuck Yeager. In 1947 he flew a rocket-powered plane that broke the sound barrier—the speed sound travels through the air. Yeager's test flight in 1947 was 700 mph (1,127 kph). Today's fastest jets can reach more than twice that speed. Yeager continued to test new planes into the 1970s, helping engineers build the best fighters possible for the Air Force.

41

WOMEN IN THE AIR FORCE

The first American woman received a license to fly a plane in 1911, but it took several decades before U.S. women flew military aircraft.

During World War II, some flew in a program called Women Airforce Service Pilots (WASP). The pilots flew planes from factories to bases and tested new models. Leading the program was Jacqueline Cochran. She had become

Jacqueline Cochran

famous before the war, winning airplane races and setting many records for speed and altitude.

It took several more decades, however, before women were allowed to enter the U.S. Air Force Academy. The first female cadets started their service in 1976. Four years later 97 women earned the rank of second lieutenant.

Martha McSally

By law, women could not hold jobs that put them directly into combat. But in 1995 Martha McSally became the first U.S. woman to fly a plane in combat over enemy territory, during a mission over Iraq. In 2004 she became the first female fighter squadron commander. Her squadron flew A-10 Thunderbolts in Afghanistan.

Eileen Collins is another female airman who made history. Collins was an Air Force flight instructor and had just finished training to be a test pilot when she joined NASA as an astronaut. She commanded the space shuttle *Columbia* on a mission to place a telescope in space in 1999. Collins was the first woman to command a space shuttle, and she did it again in 2005.

Commander Eileen Collins

WOMEN IN THE AIR FORCE

Number in 2012:	62,236
Percentage of total:	18.9
Number of officers:	12,342
Percentage of total:	19
Number of pilots:	703
Number of navigators:	263

Airmen of all backgrounds have made history with the Air Force. But most of them are not looking to be heroes. They simply want to serve their country. Their skills and dedication make the Air Force a mighty power in the skies and space.

GLOSSARY

aerial—relating to something that happens in the skies

aptitude—talent or ability to do a certain task

aviator—person trained to fly an aircraft

candidate—someone seeking to hold a certain job or title

commissioned—given authority over others by the president in order to carry out important tasks in the military

dogfight—aerial combat between planes

enlisted—joined a group, such as a branch of the military

insignia—object or symbol connected to a particular rank in the military

insurgent—person battling his or her own government

kill—an enemy plane shot down during a dogfight

meteorology—the study of the climate and changes in the weather

nuclear—energy converted by splitting two particles of matter

reconnaissance—scouting an area to see what it looks like and if it has any dangers

recruit—to seek out someone for a job, or the person who agrees to do it

satellite—object in space that circles a larger object, such as a planet

surveillance—keeping watch over people or activities that could be harmful

terrorist—person who tries to create fear by killing innocent people or destroying property as a way to gain his or her political or religious goals

SOURCE NOTES

Chapter 1: Missions in Air and Space
Page 7, line 11: *Airman: Air Force Handbook 1.* 4th ed., 2007, p. 16.
5 Nov. 2012. www.e-publishing.
af.mil/shared/media/epubs//
AFHANDBOOK1.pdf

Chapter 3: Joining the Air Force
Page 14, line 1: U.S. Air Force.
5 Nov. 2012. www.airforce.com/

**Chapter 4: Learning
The Air Force Way**
Page 18, line 17: USAF online video.
5 Nov. 2012. www.airforce.com/joining-
the-air-force/basic-military-training/

READ MORE

Dougherty, Martin J. *Air Warfare.*
Pleasantville, N.Y.: GS Learning Library, 2010.

Goldish, Meish. *Air Force: Civilian to Airman.*
New York: Bearport Publishing, 2011.

Loveless, Antony. *Fighter Pilots.* New York: Crabtree Pub. Co., 2010.

Porterfield, Jason. *USAF Special Tactics Team.*
New York: Rosen Publishing, 2008.

Schwartz, Heather E. *Women of the U.S. Air Force.*
Mankato, Minn.: Capstone Press, 2011.

INTERNET SITES

Use FactHound to find Internet sites related to this book. All of the sites on FactHound have been researched by our staff.

Here's all you do:

Visit *www.facthound.com*

Type in this code: 9780756546205

RESOURCES

U.S. Air Force
www.airforce.com/joining-the-air-force/enlisted-overview/
A site designed to start the Air Force enlistment process

U.S. Air Force
www.af.mil
The official website of the U.S. Air Force offers information and links

U.S. Air Force Academy
www.academyadmissions.com
The official website of the U.S. Air Force Academy offers information and advice

INDEX

ABOUT THE AUTHOR

Michael Burgan is the author of many books for children and young adults, both fiction and nonfiction. His works include biographies of U.S. and world leaders and histories of the American Revolution, World War II, and the Cold War. A graduate of the University

TODAY'S U.S. AIR FORCE

A jet plane soars through the sky. A drone hovers above an enemy target waiting to release its deadly rocket. A GPS satellite circles Earth, sending information that helps you get where you want to go. Behind all these activities are the men and women of the U.S. Air Force.

THE U.S. ARMED **FORCES**

Whether during wartime or peacetime, the U.S. military is ready to spring into action. The men and women of the armed forces defend and protect the United States and help those around the world who are in need. Learn more about the U.S. military and its structure, responsibilities, training, and missions.

ISBN 978-0-7565-4633-5

90000

CompassPoint**Books**
a capstone imprint www.capstonepub.com